wheeze

ee

Marcus Whale

First published 2019
by Subbed In
www.subbed.in

© Marcus Whale 2019

Book design by Michael Sun
Cover design by Dan Hogan
Original template by Sam Wieck
Text set in 8pt Domaine Text

First edition

Printed and bound in Birraranga (Melbourne)

National Library of Australia Cataloguing-in-Publication:
Whale, Marcus
wheeze / Marcus Whale.
ISBN: 978-0-6481475-5-8 (paperback)

Subbed In 006

All rights reserved.

This book is copyright. Apart from any fair dealing for the purposes of research, criticism, study, review or otherwise permitted under the Copyright Act, no part of this book may be reproduced by any process without permission. Inquiries should be addressed to Subbed In: hello@subbed.in

I grew up on Bediagal land and live on Gadigal land. These poems refer to my life in these places and I acknowledge the unceded sovereignty of those clans, and of all First Nations across this continent. Subbed In and I pay our respects to elders past and present. Always was, always will be Aboriginal land.

8	I want to be a goth
11	*The Genius of Evil* by Guillaume Geefs
14	Cities XL
17	Like Pazuzu
19	Subject is a weird word
22	Owed Nothing
25	The Kitchen/The Furnace/The Body
29	*I Try* by Macy Gray
31	Wet Couch
34	Mixtape
39	Bexley, 2005
42	11th June 1911, 31°9'N 30°21'E
44	Degrassi Plot Synopsis
48	Cave
51	Morality Is The Weakness Of The Brain

I want to be a goth

I want to be a goth.
Goths have more fun.
In my opinion, goths look great while having this fun.
I'm finally saying to you:
Be the black of my lips.
Make my lips black, actually.
Run your tongue black all around this place you've never been.
Black all around the hole.
This is called "adornment".
This is called "I am yet to tell you all of these things and I don't know why".
I'm thinking eyeliner is a kind of frame.
I'm thinking "nice" when you enter the frame.
I'm thinking being a goth is mourning all I should have been, which is more goth than being goth.
Being goth is a hole that feels endless.
Being goth is loss, which autocorrects to "kiss".
To whom and for whom, you might ask.
Is this the black of my lips?
Is this the night?
Is it tonight?
Being a goth means I can be excessive.
Being a goth is actually being a teenager, which feels like something I never was and always will be.
Your neck is white and long.
Your neck tells me we're all gonna die anyway.
I'm thinking, in this eyeliner frame, your neck is a portal.
Two tiny holes of where I'll be announce my presence.
There's blood where you'll be.
Being a goth means blood everywhere.
Being a goth, I'd have to know how to clean.
I don't know what that's like.

I've seen necks.
I've earned an eyeliner frame for this one.
But being a goth, I'm looking for new holes.
When I'm a goth, you'll be my next hole.
When I'm a goth, I'll be your hole
When I'm a goth, fill my holes.
When I'm a goth, find this hole.

The Genius of Evil by Guillaume Geefs

Trying to adjust
to night mode
'cause light

is yet to
reach his face
this morning.

On twitter
twink Lucifer
sits forlorn.

On twitter, I learn
twink Lucifer
was replaced

by otter Lucifer.
Twink Lucifer,
Hot Satan. The genius

of evil shouldn't be
this cute. Or this sad.
The posture is

kind of like
how it looks when
he's texting,

the curve of his
back, at least
at this res looking

like Lucifer's
chiropteran wings, a
shawl of bone,

a cage for light
until I wake
him up again.

Cities XL

That morning, I couldn't see the way he did.
In the photo, he's lit poorly.
When I zoom, it might as well be a stone.

        How do we learn to move?

In my reckoning it's the fear of the endless.
In my reckoning
it's only human to want more.

I'm trying to work out the distance between
this mountain or that mountain
and what that would look like imposed on
somewhere else I think I know better.
I'm trying to work out
how I would look somewhere else.
I'm trying to reckon
the endlessness of where I've never been.

On Cities XL, which is no longer compatible
with my OS,
I've made places that almost looked like this.

        How do we learn to see?

Someone I met recently has made me wish
I could still play Cities XL
& not be disappointed by the graphic renderings
of people learning to walk my streets.

Someone I met recently
would be perfect to graphically render, I reckon,
if I knew how to render.

If I knew how to render
the way I know how to see,
maybe I could tell you
how it feels to be like the almighty.

> How do we learn to know?
> How do we learn to know what we see?

In the distance between this and that mountain
is all the glow that's ever hit me,
mostly from computer monitors
and the wish to render
and the wish to be rendered
and to be not blind
at least for this time I am between mountains,
at least for this time I have spent
learning that what I see
is fleshily talking back to me,
too real
at this definition.

Now he's talking, but it's coded
and I don't see the way he sees
and beyond the smog there's some islands.
Past those islands is enough water
to let us exist far longer
than we deserve.

Like Pazuzu

One day I wanna sound like Lara Flynn Boyle
does when she says "I want you to fuck me"
to Philip Seymour Hoffman.

It's breathy, impossibly so,
more of a wheeze,
the air of sex yet to come.

They're both gone now in different ways
but the legacy, every time I watch
Queer as Folk or Tumblr with Safe Mode off,

is as certain as my need to change. Michael
searches for Brian through the backroom in
Babylon and I wonder if the moans are foley

or otherwise achieved through feats of gust.
Is it incorrect to describe a wind as
going through me? Not among

or around, but entering, via slit,
via hole. Consider me a wind tunnel.
Meanwhile, Lara is fucked, as we see

through a window and I think about
the sway of its curtain. It's sheer (chiffon
or something) so we see an abbed bod

pendulate. Possibly this bod is the air's source,
the kind of air that comes from the southwest
and runs right through like Pazuzu. Elsewhere, Justin

whispers to Brian, "I want you inside me." They're
silhouettes, they're traces, and where air cannot be
they make its shape.

Subject is a weird word

I scrolled past a photo of us and in my periphery
it looked like my ex and me in bed together,
a pic that my friend Ivan took
in a book that no one received except its subjects.

Subject is a weird word. I'm googling the
origins of why I was not referred to
as an object when a culturally powerful
older gay man had me undress for his lens,

not for a book but for a huge print
maybe bought by someone for a few k or more.
I scrolled past our photo and it seems
difficult to decode why you let me on your bed

in the same way I don't know why
I let him into my bedroom. Being an object
is like being a ghost. Being an object is like
being not there but being there,

a figment, seen and not heard. What does
it mean for your surface to be bought for a few k?
I search his name in my gmail. With a jolt I remember
he had inscribed around my navel in the print—

inscription like a naming. Naming like owning.
Subjected to ownership. In emails we're friendly
and I'm enthusiastic for his attention. Some February
I was invited to the very exhibition at which my

image was for sale. I wonder if you're
aware of your value to me. I wonder if
you've ever known the images I'm making.
I'm trying to make it so you're more than a figment

yowling out of the surface. I'm looking at posters of
things next to your bed I've wanted to be,
looking like a wish. Wishing like inscribing. Inscribing
but less than naming. An inscription with no surface.

Owed Nothing

                        It's a bit after seven and
I keep my eyes closed for the procession
       of three housemates opening the front door to
cool wind on my "sleeping" face (of which
                        I am glad)
and by the time I wake from a dream
       of a paradise island in catastrophic flood
it's hours later so maybe the wind
            is air I might have gasped for
and their footsteps the herald of
     gaping waves overwhelming a Korean shore
and still I haven't seen you
                     and still I am sweaty underneath.

You let me stay overnight and before I asked,
       I'd already thought of three different ways to say it.
Three different housemates,
   three different gulps for air.

                        Later,
I wanna tell you the thing I've been meaning to tell you and
            we both know what naming it will do
but I do it anyway.
    The word is "crush"
and the answer could be anything,
                     whatever,
   something.

Now there's nothing left to know and
              what little there is left is
not enough.

On the other hand, nothing is ever,
                really ever,
                              done.

Elsewhere, I'll still be two thumbs away
                tracing the shape of things yet to come.

Please don't feel obligated,
I'm owed nothing.

The Kitchen/
The Furnace/
The Body

There's cracks in this kitchen's concrete floor
and maybe my oesophagus if I keep this up
but they are definitely in this floor
and beneath that
and beneath that
> a rupture through about two hundred years of this.
> Buildings on building.

Land is sovereign before a state is sovereign.
The land is always being founded
> and I am still settling /
> un-emigrated /
> diasporic /
> this dysmorphic load,   like

a series of plates left on top of the speaker over here

                                                like how

I could show you the ways in which I have changed
> with a series of images.
> A motherboard
> pushing out cables,
> tentacled inside dark blue aluminium.

I might have been reminded of other places with this device.
> We were promised transit.
> We were promised landlessness.
> We made promises.
> I am making promises to what I have heard is geography.

This is a geography, or:
> This is an interval of gases, mostly nitrogen and smog.
> This is a line made from the cycles of my body
> which empties and fills
> which forms itself through the churning of desire.
> This is the house we live in,
> This is 230 years.
> This is the house desire made
> and with it we'll burn someday.

*I'm trying to find out
where kong-kong was
cremated but this city
is inscrutable to me.*

*I'm trying to find this
interval of gas as I'm
burping. He died trying
to pass something.*

*Indigestion fills me with
dread. My body is
curved over a bowl.
I'm acidic for hours.*

*His body was slid
into what I guess was
a furnace. One tube
into another. My head*

*bowed into the coloured
tag placed on my chest
to remind us that I was
his daughter's son. After,*

we ate.

> His upper body had tiny blond hairs all over
> Like the sort of down grown after starvation
> But he was just pubescent and 13
> And when he saw me looking he
> Knew I needed his validation
> And he flexed it into a series of lines

(Momentarily, like a defence
From my imaginary hands)
And so I
With my nascent body
And my in-between skin colour
(Not even as tan as his)
Mirrored the exact movement.
It was neat and clean.
It was almost a joke.
And in the Clovelly water he was
Bigger than me in all these ways
And so blond in the '02 summer
And salty-haired cause our pool was salt-based
And named after a salty-haired "Boy"
And I understood his way was the exact
Way I had ever wanted to be.

I Try by Macy Gray

Sometimes he closes his eyes instead of speaking.

I try to say goodbye and I choke.

His was the first Eurasian family in Chatswood.

Now it's gentrified.

My once-local train station will be surrounded by high rises and my mum never has any Chinese friends anymore.

The land is always being founded.

When I was twelve my mum made me cry about being bigger than the other Eurasian boys.

I had thought that maybe she did this because she was used to the smallness of Asian men.

This is an essentialist notion.

These things I have internalised.

I'm placing myself into someone else's phantom limbs.

I try to walk away and I stumble.

He is tall and my strides are like a child's.

I'm guessing he's hairless like my kong-kong.

When I was thirteen, I was so proud of my snail trail.

When I was thirteen, I had a thing for boys' asses.

He asks if he's grope-able. I can't look anywhere but his face.

When I try to hide it, it's clear.

When I try to answer, I can't even hear myself.

He looks exactly like someone on webcam in 2007.

He looks exactly like the half-Japanese cellist boy from year seven.

It is racist to think all Asians look the same.

These are things I have internalised.

When I shave, I am code switching.

His face is spotless.

Tonight I peeled a layer of skin off my forehead.

My world crumbles when you are not near.

Wet Couch

I'm outside and I can't work it out.
I'm outside and where you might have been
there is a wet couch.
How many hours will it hold water?
At this temperature?
In this climate?

Upstairs, I remember this amount of skin differently,

>   it's been something like five years
>   but who's counting,

things that have changed hang off us,
but I still feel like this is exactly like
when my parents weren't home
for a few days in 2006,

>   something bled on the screen
>   and he said something about
>   the revolution that ensues &
>   I only think of his white belly
>   and a small river of cum.

The things that have changed.

I don't know how to sing this one.
I am making silences for you
to read into.
I am making silences.

>   Elsewhere they're holes,
>   waterholes and somewhere
>   else a couch floods

because there's nothing to say, really.

Afterwards we're almost asleep but your phone goes off in the corner.

                                        This is the second
                                        time in two days.

Tomorrow it'll be dry again,   Tomorrow
I might let you open a door on me again, I might let you
& this time I'll be the reservoir.   dry me up.

I first saw you in my bedroom   Tomorrow
and I thought your bowl was neat   I might
and I said something   dry
incomprehensible   my feet
and I thought something else.   at your door.

Mixtape

1

Spacetime by Tinashe is playing when his stoned body's aura fills my room. In the breakdown, my sweat enters his mouth, at least via vapours we share, or at least telekinetically, I think while also thinking: "You can stay here tonight". His aura says something but I can't quite hear because my speakers are kinda trebly. Outside on the porch a cloud forms for a sec.

2

I see him for the first time in two years but I'm pretty much sure it's *Happy Nation* by Ace of Base being cut off along with the engine of his car and I'm reminded of the "base of aces" in Lorient and the fascistic dirge that was murmuring underneath my street's endless traffic moments before I decided to just watch him saunter down the street unbothered by any of this.

3

It's this jazz event but they're not playing jazz except this one group who are some mostly white version of a New Orleans brass band circa 2016 circa Australia. After the set, *Next Lifetime* by Erykah Badu comes on and this saxophonist who looks like a celestial body invites me through the window of this bar. It's what cherubim call an Aether Portal. I'd say the song was soundtracking our epic transit through the virtual core of my imagination but then I remember that the shape of cherubim can't even be speculated. Later, I follow his Instagram and it's almost the same except every time I see him in person now there's a burnt black hole in my vision.

4

It's been months now so we can joke about it but at some point the version of him I conjure when *Visions of Gideon* by Sufjan Stevens comes over my speakers was definitely more real than the amalgam of flesh beside me. At home, I receive and send messages over four possible platforms, which are like the points of a compass. After triangulating our position, a kind of ghost appears through the video screen. This one talks back but in my vision he's rendered in a kind of silicone casing that when spread over his entire body looks more like an eye. My dad used to ask if I were the son of a glassmaker but that look he gives me is the most opaque thing I have ever seen.

Bexley, 2005

We're at the creek.
Your friends are not my friends.
The pool is nearby.
I think you're the nicest person I could imagine.
I think you're so nice I still don't know what you really think of me.
I don't remember this driveway.
I don't remember this white palace veneer.
Is that sociopathic?
That I don't understand how you don't need anything from me?
This valley is different on the other side, down the hill from Red Rooster.
I'm embarrassed that I don't know Cantonese.
I like it when you allow me to confess things about myself.
We smoke something from some guy at Ashfield Boys.
You say you feel nothing and so do I but I'm also not sure of your subtext.
Willow branches pour from where we are into the water.
I enjoy exorcising shame, which as a process is much like creating it.
Bigger exhales make the creek look like a Louisiana swamp.
If I understood better, I'd ask you to breathe into my mouth.
If I knew better, I'd find the point at which your voice resonates my whole body.
The creek is full of shit.
My future boyfriend will describe me as flow.
My future boyfriend will describe being poured through the gaps between my fingers.
If only I could know that my body is a tube.
The creek hasn't flooded in years.

If only you could need me the way I need you.
I might know how it feels to drink from a river's mouth.
There isn't enough time for me to walk you home.
Time enters the space between us like a whirlpool, or a wormhole.
You say you enjoy our time together.
Further on, the creek becomes a canal.
I could pretty much just eat your nose.
The best thing I can be is open like you, every little pore cleaned.
You enter the hole and I row a boat upstream.

11th June 1911, 31°9'N 30°21'E

Out of extraterrestrial rubble,
an impression of a thing
that might have been alive once
(4.5 billion years ago, somewhere else.)

Out of the rubble,
this un-human murmuring.
Some *thing* remains—
not the dog, incinerated on impact

so severely that it might
never have existed.
Nor is it Martian nano-bacterial cultures
incepting Earthlife in the Proterozoic era

since what is a fossil but a
clue ready to become a myth?
It's nothing more than the light,
the impossible hover of angelic light

Sometimes looking like your face
mired with glow,
that murmur, a map.
Sometimes it's a look,

the invocation, a horror, the lonely
immersion of being too much to know
with nothing but a fossil for evidence.
Nothing more than an unknowable thing.

No more than the impossible
thing of knowing the exact
sound you'll make when I
tell you what you already know.

Degrassi Plot Synopsis

1

Maya submerges herself in bathwater. The angle recalls Britney's *Everytime* video such that I wonder if she'll return to the surface, which Britney does. The shot lingers—enough to notice my own breath—how it might feel to be under, unbreathing, the world above smeared.

2

She's just a pair of eyes as autoplay delivers disaster porn. I think I see a tornado or maybe a cyclone but it's become a blur of trauma and I'm sure it's the same for her. Suddenly it's morning and she wonders about the abyss of time that she'd poured herself into like so many ruptures in the earth's crust.

3

Next season, Maya is treated with excessive delicacy by all of her friends until she can't remember how it felt to be more than a ghost.

4

Her sister Katie sometimes makes guest appearances separated by maybe a season or two or three. We wonder what her life might be like off-screen. The thought that many seasons ago she might have done something cruel to someone repeatedly hangs over her sweetness in these appearances. But it is too long ago to know for sure.

5

The past is the endless rolling of seasons. The past is being able to measure intervals of time as queer characters, or ships, or consent storylines. The past is streamable, unlawfully.

6

Jimmy forever.

Cave

He had begun to stage his own death.
A cave and the soft
pawing of a big cat; I am no longer
sure of which species.

In this vision,
he has enough time
to assume lotus
before his jugular is eviscerated.
Staged, dreamed,

but I understand
that my nose
has a feline quality,

that I have always eroticised
the neck, that sinewy
tube of meat, heavy
on the gristle, his apple
hard as bone.

In the text
he used the word
"gladly",

which when placed
beside this dream
is a reminder
or a warning that
the saliva in my mouth
is the same temperature as blood.

Concentrating hard I
enter the cave, hungry
after days of nothing.

I am muscular, slinky
and furred. Desperate,
I sniff him out and
imagine how this
might taste.

I gaze at his neck and desire
runs through my whole length.

I am trying to remember
how it felt
before any of this.

I am trying to remember
the exact smell, the lick,
the slick hand,
the sleight,
when I entered.

Morality Is The Weakness Of The Brain

1

We focus on their faces in half light.
Past us is smoke, or an aura.
One secretly crosses their fingers inside a hoodie.
The other thinks about her wetness under thermals.
The location's unknowable to us. It might be a vacant lot
or a carpark.
But it's light enough to see what might become of them.
I'm almost ready, we hear one of them say. It's like a prayer.
In the distance: some atmos sound that might have
been a train once.

2

Together they make a shape like an upside down T.
It's hard to tell but we assume their faces are filled
with longing.
Their hair covers her face like a curtain. *B, I can't see.
Oh, sorry.* Light catches the smooth lustre of B's chest.
They gaze hard at something beyond our frame.
I'm close, says one of their voices.
Blue mist settles like a third body around them.
Above, a clear moon.

3

We assume one of them faked it. But we're not sure why.
On a grassy landing, she cleans her fingers of saliva & ass.
They walk a while 'til they hit a road.
The road stretches behind them and they're unspeaking.
The promise of sun discretely changes the white balance.
They finally talk, but it's about tomorrow and it's about other places.
A bike appears beside her. *I'm tired. I'm gonna split.*
We see her exit the scene with a kind of melancholy. It's untouchable, we think.

4

Everything's still weird.
Houses border our view on either side.
We hear the uneven rhythm of B's gait against the road.
We focus on a sine wave cycle of new lights on their face.
From the yellow, we know they're not LED.
In this way, B walks for several minutes.
They stop, seeming weary.
Actually, they receive a text.

5

B glows under the streetlight.
Over some time, its yellow is blown out by the sun's more yellow yellow.
B assumes the posture of waiting, which we reckon kind of resembles a gargoyle.
At full dawn, they disappear from view.
From a new angle, one of the street's houses seems to pulse orange.
Incense makes a subtle stream from a side window.
To our right, the sound of low voices in rhythm.
Across the street, bins roll. Over the curve, bikes, cars, birds, other places.

6

We follow with quietness the route B might have taken.
The movement's slow, steady, as if we're hunting.
We pass through a driveway bound by brick on either side.
Windows painted closed.
Everything's louder here.
Through a pane we see a structure we'll silently name an altar.
Something like five women (and maybe more we can't see) form a canopy of heads.
In the centre B is prostrate, lit by fire.

////////

7

Sun hits their eyes.
They're under a sheet, alone and dreaming.
It could be any time of day, really.
Towards the edge there's a huge, open book.
Feels like they were born inside of it.
We zoom in on the book slowly, their body warping with the angle.
We notice the length of their fingers, thumbing the edge of some word.
It all seems incomprehensible.

8

It's the same day and outside.
That girl from before plays with her fingers under the light.
She's different from yesterday but we don't know why.
We track to see B beside her.
They don't speak to each other immediately—not the way you'd expect.
I know what you want.
B is expressionless but it feels performed.
It seems like she might continue but there isn't anymore to say.

9

Later that day, B burrows into an untidy corner of their room.
B adorns themself with the thought of their first meeting.
The room melts into another room, bluer and more populated.
Their eyes deploy a path through the air to her beyond a dozen unstable faces.
Their connection becomes real. She stares. Backlit. Outside. She's puzzled. *What did you do in there?*
There's heaps I can show you but I'm not allowed. They don't understand us.
Generationally, I mean.

10

A stylus circuits a runout groove.
We pull out to see the slow movement of B in their daily practice.
They're kneeling on the bed, facing away, so the invocation is not intelligible to us.
It looks like the first flight of a juvenile magpie.
They seem impossibly thin for a time.
The city's yawning air presses through a gap in the window.
B turns. Something levitates.
We think it might be a trick of the light. We think maybe we don't understand.

11

Don't know why these things happen.
I forget who I am.
Make me more than my body.
I'm praying that you'll know me.
I can't know myself in this way.
I can't stop looking at where you've been.
They set a dark blue object on the stool beside them.
From the left, out of the dark, a glow emerges.

////////

12

B's folded neatly in bed, gazing offscreen.
We track birdseye over their naked length.
Joining them from our right is a third person we've yet to see until now.
They kiss like they both know what just happened.
B mounts her in a way we've seen before. *Once more?*
She must know what this means, we think.
After some time with no response, B melts beside her, spooning.
She rolls over so they form a circle, facing. *Tell me from the start.*

13

We view them both tighter now, each in their own shot.
Their eyes are blue and grey. *She has an aura.*
There's more to say but she looks opaque, not understanding.
When I met her I wasn't like this. B gestures to their body.
She pulls closer, into B's nape. *Maybe she's afraid.*
I can't take her with me. So what's the point?
She runs her fingers along B's brow. *Of the transit?*
Of the transit. And any of the practice, which we know is everything.

14

The sun's angle is long against the bed so we know it's later.
Do you think you're ready for this? She shields her eyes.
B stares directly upward as if there is no ceiling. Yes.
There's nothing left.
The whole room is in view as they both slide off the bed.
Its clutter appears ornate in the light as they fill two bags with many objects.
By the time they're done we understand this room has become another room.
When they leave it is owned by something else.

15

B and the third person are tracked from behind.
Golden light in front of them blackens them into silhouettes.
They talk but we only hear the roar of cars beside them on the road.
A white van slowly follows beside them, pulls over.
Its door slides open and they throw their bags and themselves inside.
The shot becomes still. The footpath is empty for a time.
We linger, gazing at its form. We understand.
It is clear they won't be seen here again.

16

It's night and we see the city from above.
Outlines of places we suppose we've seen form a glowing map.
For a moment a house flashes brighter than all the others.
The sound of their chanting gradually overwhelms the atmos.
To our left is a plume of smoke rising rapidly in a column, lit by moonlight.
From what seems like inside us, a light opens into the column.
The glow rises inexorably toward us.
The light swallows everything.

ACKNOWLEDGEMENTS

Thank you to Dan Hogan, Victoria Manifold, Jared Richards, Angela Garrick and Marcus Thaine for their help and support around the writing of this book.

ABOUT THE AUTHOR

Marcus Whale is a musician and artist working on Gadigal land. He has made music as part of groups Collarbones and BV, as well as work under his own name, releasing the album *Inland Sea* in 2016.

As a performer in a visual art context, his works are mostly produced in collaboration with other artists including Athena Thebus and Eugene Choi. These works mine mythologies of longing and shame, often appropriating the high drama of religious ritual.

Forming a companion to this performance work, he has a writing practice across poetry, fiction and non-fiction, including *Devotionals*, a debut collection of poems published by Ruin Press in 2015.

ABOUT SUBBED IN

Subbed In is a not-for-profit DIY literary organisation and small press based in Sydney, Australia. Subbed In's program of publications and events aim to elevate the voices of trans people, people of colour, non-binary people, sex workers, women, people with a disability, LGBTQIA+ people, First Nations people, survivors, working class people, and anyone who finds themselves on the margins of the supremely white, cis, heteronormative, capitalist, colonial, ableist, patriarchal hellscape in which we live.

For more information visit: *www.subbed.in*

ALSO AVAILABLE FROM SUBBED IN

When I die slingshot my ashes onto the surface of the moon
by Jennifer Nguyen

HAUNT (THE KOOLIE)
by Jason Gray

The Hostage
by Šime Knežević

If you're sexy and you know it slap your hams
by Eloise Grills

blur by the
by Cham Zhi Yi

Parenthetical Bodies
by Allison Gallagher

The Naming
by Aisyah Shah Idil

Girls and Buoyant
by Emily Crocker